UNLOCKING
the Measure of
FAITH

Realizing Your Full Potential in Christ

RICHARD BROWN III

DEDICATION

I dedicate this book to my lifelong best friend
and companion, my wife Clara.

Clara's greatest gift to me is her love and passion for
Christ. She is a shining example to everyone of what
it means to be a follower of Jesus Christ. Your love
motivates and inspires me. Your heart is in my heart.

ACKNOWLEDGMENTS

First, I acknowledge my Lord and Savior Jesus Christ; without His grace I could do nothing of significance or importance. Because Jesus died for me, I now live for Him.

To my parents, Richard and Eunice Brown, although they are no longer with us, I know that they would be proud of this milestone in my life.

In memory of my godly grandparents John and Loretta Toller and my great grandmother Gertrude Gentry who took me to church as a child and instilled godly principles in my life.

To my Aunts Lola Toller, Marcella Leftwich and my big brother John Toller II, three of my early role models who believed in me when I didn't believe in myself.

A special thanks to my two lovely daughters DeDe Dotson and Candace Johnson who patiently prayed for me while their mother and I served as pastors and missionaries in Japan and Asia for nearly thirty years.

To Bishop Curtis Brown, Highways & Hedges Revival Center, New Bern, NC for having faith in me as a minister of Jesus Christ.

To Bishop Virgil D. Patterson, Sr., my spiritual father, pastor and friend, who has demonstrated to me what it means to be a father and a man of God.

To the former members and leaders of Agape Fellowship Ministries International, Okinawa, Japan, of which I was privileged to pastor and serve for so many years. Thank you for your commitment, dedication, and support.

To Richard and Debbie William and all of the History Maker International friends and partners across Asia and the world, thank you for your prayers, inspiration and support.

Finally, to the many pastors and leaders who serve God's people in Okinawa, Japan, thank you and continue to advance the kingdom of God.

ENDORSEMENTS

I am delighted to recommend, *Unlocking the Measure of Faith*. It is the most spiritual, deeply practical and provoking book that will impact and transform your adventure in faith. The Global Church is at a crossroad, and I believe this book sets the demarcation line between those who will do great things for God and those who will maintain the status quo. If you read this, it will change your life, your future and your ministry. For a generation seeking to take your city for Christ this is a must read.

Dr. Richard William
International Director/Senior Pastor
History Maker International Church
Singapore

Unlocking the Measure of Faith addresses one of the most critical topics in the body of Christ today; FAITH! We live in a world where the modern church has placed so much emphasis on the visible that many members of the body of Christ do not even try to unlock their measure of faith. However, this dynamic book takes us back to the original intent of the "seed form faith" that God has dealt to us. I issue a challenge to you today. If you desire to engage in the work of the ministry and not just be a good church attendee, then you need to read this book so that you can begin to unlock the measure of faith that God has given to you.

Kenneth A. Lester
Pastor, Agape Christians In Action
Jacksonville, North Carolina

Unlocking the Measure of Faith is very intriguing and will challenge readers to evaluate their faith, purpose and commitment to Christ. The author integrates wisdom and personal experiences to express unprecedented truths, which will aid readers to live an effective Christian life. This book is a must read, and a catalyst for transformation. I highly recommend this book to all leaders and congregants.

Michael D. Odom, Jr.
Apostle, Senior Pastor
Agape Christian Worship Center
Albany, Georgia

It is with great excitement that I endorse this phenomenal book, *Unlocking the Measure of Faith* by Richard Brown III. This book is well written, informative and practical. He comes straight out the gate to let readers know that there is a fundamental problem with our faith. As he states in the book, "In America I find it somewhat amazing that the 'consumer-minded' Christian shops for churches in much the same manner as we shop for goods and services." We must hit the reset button and go back to biblical faith where we view our devotion and service to the Lord Jesus Christ supreme.

Unlocking the Measure of Faith will change your views and identify your measure of faith. If the reader would apply the principles in this powerful book they will transform nations for the kingdom of God.

Dr. Jeffery Chapman, Sr.
Senior Pastor
Raleigh North Christian Center
Raleigh, North Carolina

CONTENTS

INTRODUCTION

Jesus left the church with a seemingly impossible mission, "Go ... and make disciples of all the nations" (Matt. 28:19). However, with this mission He apportioned to every man, "the measure of faith" (Rom. 12:3).

In this book I share insights, wisdom, truths and experiences designed to encourage those who are daring enough to accept Christ's call to participate in transforming the nations of the earth for the kingdom of God. We have received our commission, our orders are clear, but what gifts, abilities and tools have we been given that will enable us to be effective in accomplishing so great a mission? I believe *Unlocking the Measure of Faith* will assist you in determining where you are best suited to function in the body of Christ and how you can unlock the potential of Christ's gift in you. Perhaps, as senior leadership in a church, this book will aid you in helping those you lead to identify their role, function and place in the local church.

In this book I will attempt to address three areas of great importance:

1. Identifying your measure of faith—When a believer recognizes that he or she has something of value to add to the body of Christ, they are more likely to remain involved and invested. Identifying our gifts also requires the involvement of senior leaders whose role it is to confirm and affirm gifts and abilities in the lives of other believers. These leaders have already demonstrated the necessary wisdom, character and experience and are not intimidated by or in competition with those they are called to disciple.

2. Developing your measure of faith—Gaining the necessary experience and wisdom to administer our gifts, callings and ministries effectively. This includes teaching, training and education through formal, traditional and non-traditional methods. Internships or apprenticeships may be necessary in order to allow for extended periods of instruction, demonstration and application. This method also affords an opportunity for character to mature in concert with the gifts.

3. Activating your measure of faith—There must be opportunities for the believer to exercise his or her gifts on a consistent basis. When the believer is consistently engaged in ministry, he or she will find fewer opportunities for distraction and boredom. Thus, the believer is transformed from a spectator into a participator in the kingdom of God.

Prayerfully, as you read this book you will become enlightened to the importance of engaging both the clergy or five-fold ministers and the layperson in works of intensified ministry. As the two co-labor together in ministry, the local church maximizes its opportunities for fulfilling the Great Commission.

I will address our responsibility as Christian leaders for making disciples our primary mission as opposed to building mega ministries or churches first. The issue is not whether or not we lead large or small congregations, but rather whether we are making disciples for Christ. Leaders build people, not churches. I will ask the tough question; is there enough Christ in the average believer who attends our services to make a difference for the kingdom of God? I will provide answers to this and other tough questions throughout this book.

Finally, you will be challenged to dream big again, to risk it all for the purpose of bringing glory and honor to our Lord and Savior Jesus Christ. If you have failed at past attempts at realizing your full potential in Christ, you will be inspired to try again. Keep in mind, Jesus didn't choose His disciples from the religious institutions of the day. He chose the unlikely. God used a shepherd boy to slay a giant (David), a murderer to deliver a nation (Moses), and an adulteress to evangelize an entire city (the woman at the well). God can use you!

Richard Brown III
Jacksonville, North Carolina

FOREWORD

Apostle Richard Brown III has boldly challenged all believers to release the shackles of religious faith and embrace the grace of one's measure given by Almighty God. In carefully reading and consciously meditating on each powerful chapter, I personally was able to capture the heartbeat of one having lived what has been recorded in *Unlocking the Measure of Faith*.

My son, Richard Brown, is powerfully presenting scriptural assurances in strengthening your faith through the realization that strong faith is attainable and expected by our Lord and Savior Jesus Christ as we journey through this pilgrimage called life. You will be tried, tested and strengthened as you are presented with a heavenly download of spiritual authority available just for the asking. I am so honored to write the foreword to a life changing, spirit filled key to life.

Dr. Virgil D. Patterson, Sr.
Bishop, Senior Pastor
Crusade Christian Faith Center
Los Angeles, California

1

THE PROBLEM WITH OUR FAITH

"Learning to believe God through another person's experience is one of the most difficult, yet
important, lessons in life."[1]   – Bill Johnson

Many books have been written defining faith and
describing with great detail what it means to
have faith in God. The Word of Faith Movement during
the 1970's and 1980's taught the church the importance
of speaking and confessing the Word of God consistently and played a vital role in helping the believer to
understand and incorporate faith into our lives as a doc-
trine or teaching. Thus, I will not attempt to define faith
as much as I will address its importance in the life of
the believer both as the distinguishing characteristic of
those who believe in Christ and the Gospel and as that
biblical or spiritual attribute that enables the believer to

experience fruitful and effective lives and ministry in the service of our Lord.

Paul states it this way:

> For I am not ashamed of the gospel, for it is the power of God for salvation to everyone who believes, to the Jew first and also to the Greek. For in it the righteousness of God is revealed from *faith* to *faith*; as it is written, But the righteous man shall live by *faith*.
> — Romans 1:16,17 (emphasis mine)

Here, Paul reveals that God is not interested in a one time, isolated act of faith at the new birth or conversion as our Western gospel often seems to suggest, but rather a "faith from start to finish." A living faith that remains active from the moment of salvation until we are finally with the Lord. A faith so powerful and alive that it transforms the entire man to the degree that faith becomes a lifestyle or way of life.

Unfortunately, our "gospel of faith" suggests that since we are justified by this one time act of faith, our justification or legal standing with God is secure and our relationship to God through Christ is complete. This mindset or thinking dismisses a very important aspect of the salvation experience called "sanctification." It is true justification sets the believer in right standing with God (see Romans 5:1), but justification is only the beginning of the process, and if justification is the "starting line" then complete or final sanctification is the "finish line."

Faith from start to finish makes God the object of our faith daily; this is, in fact, what I would call biblical faith. Biblical faith is measured by our *daily* trust, reliance and confidence in Jesus Christ and His Word. Of course, I grew up in America where too many Christians have based their faith on what we drive, where we live and how big and successful we appear to be (America has an obsession with bigness). One of the reasons for the Financial Crisis of 2008 was that too many of us were trying to live beyond our means. If my neighbor bought a new SUV then I needed to buy one bigger and newer than his. If he bought a new three-bedroom house, then even though I didn't need a larger house I had to prove that I had *faith* for a five-bedroom house. Soon, everyone was trying to achieve their version of "the American dream" without taking into account the consequences. We incurred more debt than we could afford as a country and thus followed a financial melt-down, and Christians were just as much responsible for this problem as were unbelievers. I will address this issue in more depth later in this book.

Western societies tend to rely on education, intellect, rationale and logic alone. To know and understand God, to discern God, requires participation of both spirit and intellect simultaneously. Spirit is the means by which God reveals Himself and communes with man. "God is spirit, and those who worship Him must worship in spirit and truth" (John 4:24). Likewise, faith is a spirit attribute. Faith originates with God.

Solomon wrote, "Trust in the Lord with all thine heart; and lean not unto thine own understanding" (Proverbs 3:5 KJV). To trust the Lord means to have confidence in and rely on Him, this requires faith.

Paul when addressing the Corinthians said:

And my language and my message were not set forth in persuasive (enticing and plausible) words of wisdom, but they were in demonstration of the [Holy] Spirit and power [a proof by the Spirit and power of God, operating on me and stirring in the minds of my hearers the most holy emotions and thus persuading them], So that your faith might not rest in the wisdom of men (human philosophy), but in the power of God.
                                                    – I Corinthians 2:4, 5 AMP

This is faith that becomes a true spiritual conviction in the heart of man and thus intertwines and permeates the fabric of the believer's life and produces a lifestyle of faith.

Twenty-four years of leading a church in Okinawa, Japan taught me that we have a fundamental problem with our faith: Doctrines and teaching that make keys and formulas the object of our faith rather than God Himself are a danger to true biblical Christianity.

Further, every believer has received "the measure of faith" in proportion to his or her place, function and purpose in the body of Christ for kingdom impact and success. This measure of faith is not based on personal performance, works, status or man's abilities, but rather the will and purposes of Father God. This gift of faith from God, coupled with redeemed man's obedience and desire to fulfill his God-ordained assignment for the kingdom of God produces corresponding fruit.

James teaches us that where there is genuine faith, there are works (evidence). What evidence? Houses, cars, SUVs, bling, money? Certainly not. May I suggest that the true measure of our faith is our devotion and service to our Lord, which manifests in righteousness, joy, peace, sanctification, holiness, mercy, grace, salvations, healings, ministries, disciples, etc?

James says:

"Even so faith, if it has no works, is dead, being by itself." James 2:17 NASB

Simply, if one plants an apple seed, he expects to grow an apple tree. Similarly, if one professes faith in Christ, then he should have corresponding fruit, or in this case, works. The real issue for the Western church is developing a daily, living faith in Jesus Christ and not in our dreams, visions or desires. We must resist the tendency of becoming a success driven, formula speaking and mechanical church. The object of real Christian faith must always be Jesus Christ, He is "the author and perfecter of faith" Hebrews 12:2.

There is a *strange* dichotomy being taught in our churches today that suggests that it is okay for an individual to be "saved" (possess salvation) and yet choose not to produce fruit for the kingdom of God, in other words, to continue to live a life for "self" (indulging one's own personal desires) without ever participating in the personal sanctification process that enables a believer to produce spiritual fruit for the kingdom of God.

True, there are personal advantages to becoming a follower of Jesus Christ, however, Jesus said, "But seek first His kingdom and His righteousness; and these things shall be added to you" (Matthew 6:33). As we grow and mature spiritually in Christ, we learn that fulfillment is achieved when we choose to put Him first.

The pulpit was not designed primarily as a place for men to peddle or promote "the good life" or prosperity, but rather to preach faith in Jesus Christ, redemption through His blood and the forgiveness of sins. For sure, we desire to live well and desire to see our parishioners live well, but we can ill afford to allow our faith to be defined by the things we possess.

The problem with our faith is that we have raised a generation of believers who were led to believe that God and the church exist primarily to meet their "felt needs" in order to fill the pews, as opposed to a people who exist to worship their God and serve at His pleasure.

This is what John wrote concerning the church and the bride in Revelation:

"Let us rejoice and be glad and give the glory to Him, for the marriage of the Lamb has come and His bride has made herself ready"
(Revelation 19:7).

The bride is symbolic of the church (the saints) matured, prepared and ready to meet the bridegroom, Jesus. It is time for those of us who wear the titles to take the lead in devoting ourselves to discipleship, mentoring, training and equipping this generation; taking the time and effort to walk beside them as they identify their role, function and place in the body of Christ. Reassuring those who follow our example that God will do greater works through their lives and ministries as they learn through faith and obedience to submit to Almighty God.

The church is living beneath her privilege. We took a faith that was meant to rout principalities and evil rulers, raise the dead, heal the sick and cast out demons and transformed it into a faith whose primary goal is houses, cars and bling.

The following is an example of Old Testament faith. These believers weren't even filled with the Holy Spirit:

> "And what more shall I say? For time will fail me if I tell of Gideon, Barak, Samson, Jephthah, of David and Samuel and the prophets, who by faith conquered kingdoms, performed acts of righteousness, obtained promises, shut the mouths of lions, quenched the power of fire, escaped the edge of the sword, from weakness were made strong, became mighty in war, put foreign armies to flight." (Hebrews 11:32–34)

This is just a small sampling of the impact these believers made as a result of their trust, reliance and confidence in God. How much more will we who have inherited such a sacred trust through the blood of Jesus' cross, His Word and the power of His Holy Spirit accomplish any less?

I believe the Holy Spirit is standing by, waiting for those who are daring enough to activate *the measure of faith* and perform great exploits in the earth.

I ask you to consider these words:

> [F]rom whom the whole body, being fitted and held together by that which *every* joint supplies, according to the proper working of each individual part, causes the growth of the body for the building up of itself in love.
> – (Ephesians 4:16) (italics mine).

Paul, writing to the church at Ephesus, reveals that although every believer is uniquely gifted in Christ, we were designed to function as a body, adding our individual abilities, gifts and faith to the whole so that the body is lacking nothing. This produces major challenges to a society that celebrates "rugged individualism" and independence over unity and oneness. A key to realizing our full potential in Christ is to understand that our individual gifts and ministries were given to us for one purpose—to edify the body of Christ.

Unfortunately, we live in a society that rewards self-centeredness and spiritual immaturity and values gifts and talent over Christian character. For example, an extremely gifted and talented musician joins the praise team at a local church. As a member of the team, he is expected to learn the style and flow of the praise team and add his gift accordingly. The brother becomes irritated and offended because he is required to submit his gift to the needs of the team. As a result, the brother begins to sow seeds of division among the members of the praise team. Soon, the team is divided and the brother influences others to leave and attend another church with him. Upon arriving at the new ministry he is immediately accepted as a member of the praise team. Thus he is rewarded for his rebellion and spiritual immaturity.

As we approach the return of our Lord and Savior Jesus Christ, we are learning the value of strength through faith and obedience and that the best gifts are those totally surrendered and submitted to Christ.

2

FOLLOWING JESUS DAILY – DISCIPLESHIP

"I told them the evidence of being a follower of Jesus is following Jesus. I told them believing the right things was not enough; the faith Jesus taught and lived includes behavioral evidence."[2]

— Bill Hull

Thus far in my Christian walk, I have had the privilege and esteemed honor of worshipping and representing Jesus Christ on four of the seven continents of the world. In each case, I have been able to set aside the natural, carnal and cultural differences from continent to continent because my goal is always to encounter and present the God of the Bible and not some other superficial experience. When our goal is to demonstrate the culture of the kingdom of God, every man, regardless of his background, ethnicity or status in life, is afforded the opportunity to be changed in the presence of the Lord.

In America I find it somewhat amazing that the "consumer-minded" Christian shops for churches in much the same manner as we shop for goods and services. We live in a consumer-driven society. You ask, why is this problematic? The believer's goal is to become Spirit-filled and Spirit-led, not to be driven by selfish and worldly impulses, cravings or desires. Consumerism is a friend of the flesh and enemy of the Spirit. Our culture has taught us to use our "faith" to get "stuff." This method of thinking appears to me to be contrary to Bible teaching. When true biblical principles are incorporated into the life of the believer, they produce Christian character and eternal fruit.

Sadly, too many "would be" Christians are in search of a "cultural" experience more than an encounter with Christ. Denomination, style, ethnic and racial make-up, oh, and lest I forget, convenience have become the primary factors in determining what church to attend or join. Here is a sampling of "frequently asked questions" when inviting someone to church: How long is the service? Is it a Baptist church? Is it a "black" church? Do I have to wear a suit? Do the people speak in tongues? How big is your church (how many people attend the services)? Does your church have a "good" praise team or choir? Do you have children's church? Do I have to give an offering?

Again, these are just examples, but rarely does anyone inquire about the presence of God, the Word of God, or the Holy Spirit. It seems more emphasis is placed on the culture of the people and church than on the substance and presence of God in the people. A church should be measured by the measure of Christ operating in and through the life of every believer in that particular church and whether the kingdom of God is being established and making an impact in the communities where we live and serve.

Culture, as important as it is to man, is of little importance to God (culture: the customary beliefs, social forms, and material traits of a racial, religious, social group). In fact the believer, as a result of the "new birth," has become a citizen of heaven or the kingdom of God (Ephesians 2:19). At a minimum, as kingdom agents or ambassadors for Christ, we all have been commissioned to carry out the ministry of reconciliation (II Corinthians 5:18–20).

Discipleship, because it is designed to make followers of Christ as opposed to satisfying the selfish desires of man, is our surest way of fulfilling "the Great Commission" (Matthew 28:19–20).

In our churches I find that discipleship, a serious commitment to following Jesus daily, is just another of many programs offered to our church members or attendees and at best is only offered to ease our conscience as pastors. What this tells me is that we will perpetuate the status quo of making low-commitment believers for an assignment from God that requires the highest commitment. By far, we have the finest state-of-the-art facilities, including coffee bars, bookstores, gymnasiums, multi-purpose rooms, boardrooms, rehearsal halls, nurseries, daycares, fellowship halls, parking lot shuttles, pastor and staff offices and more. We have traditional services, "seeker" services, youth services, singles services, Friday, Saturday and Sunday services, "dress down" services, "dress up" services and not to mention the finest conferences, workshops, and Christian and Gospel concerts. However, all too often, I find one thing lacking ... *discipleship.*

Discipleship is the "on purpose," deliberate, intentional, planned process of equipping and training believers through demonstration to imitate the life, character and ministry of Jesus Christ daily. Jesus did not intend for His church to become merely a religious or social function people participate in once or twice a week to live "the good life" and then go to heaven. As church leaders we must not only concern ourselves with making converts and filing seats for church growth, but more importantly to make disciples who are capable of making more followers of Christ. Many of us can recall a time when we participated in a six-week, or maybe at best three-month, discipleship program in our churches as young or new converts. Upon completing the program we were likely recognized at a Sunday morning service where we were then assimilated into the general membership of the church and left to continue our Christian walk on our own as best we could. Even now, when we hear the term discipleship we think to ourselves, "oh I've already completed that program."

Today, the six-week discipleship program has been replaced by the "new members" class. This class is usually nothing more than an orientation to the methods, vision and beliefs of that particular local body. Few churches may have a "new convert" or "new believers" class, but there is little beyond these classes that consistently and systematically prepares the believer to become productive members of the body of Christ or kingdom of God.

Jesus said to His disciples:

"If anyone wishes to come after me, let him deny himself, and take up his cross *daily,* and follow me."

— (Luke 9:23) (italics mine)

I've learned that the key to being an effective Christian is following Jesus daily, and through following Jesus daily we experience effective ministry, purpose and vision. One of the primary disciplines of discipleship is *renewing the mind.*

Paul said this:

I urge you therefore, brethren, by the mercies of God, to present your bodies a living and holy sacrifice, acceptable to God, which is your spiritual service of worship.

— Romans 12:1

In order to follow Jesus daily we must recognize His legal right (Lordship) over our lives. To an American this probably sounds too much like slavery. Well, in a manner of speaking, that is exactly what it is. The writer of Romans however, reminds us of just how lost we were and how Jesus suffered for our sins upon the cross and how through His grace we have been redeemed and reconciled to Father God. Therefore, as an act of love and gratitude to our God and Father, we ought to offer our lives in His service.

Again, Paul said:

And do not be conformed to this world, but be transformed by the renewing of your mind, that

you may prove what the will of God is, that which
is *good* and *acceptable* and *perfect*.
                                    – Romans 12:2 (Italics mine).

The mind of the believer must be *completely* over-
hauled. In other words our thinking must change. In
America we're taught, "be a winner," "be number one,"
"whatever it takes be a success," "if it feels good do
it," "have it your way," and last but not least "you have
rights." As we read, study, hear and meditate on the
Word of God, our minds are being renewed. During
this process, the Holy Spirit begins to reveal the will
of God for our lives. I cannot overstate the importance
of yielding to the Holy Spirit as He reveals the Father
and Son to us. Some have said "God has three wills,
good, acceptable and perfect." A more accurate depic-
tion of God's will is that, as we learn to follow Jesus
daily through the highs and lows of life, we begin to
recognize that God's one will for us is always, only
good, acceptable and perfect. We learn to see God's
will for our lives through His eyes and not through natural eyes. It is utterly impossible for the human mind
to fathom God's plan for our lives and ministry in the
natural without the aid of the Holy Spirit.

The letter to the Corinthians said this:

Things which eye has not seen and ear has not
heard, and which have not entered the heart of
man, all that God has prepared for those who
love Him. For to us God revealed them through
the Spirit; for the Spirit searches all things, even
the depths of God.   – I Corinthians 2:9–10

Jesus never commissioned any of His disciples or apostles to build the church, but He did tell them to make disciples (Matthew 28:19).

Daily Disciplines

During my early Christian development I was blessed to come into the acquaintance of two key Christian brothers, Jerry Kinard and Robert Dotson. Together, along with my wife Clara, we determined to encourage one another through fellowship, prayer, witnessing and the Word of God (not necessarily in that order). As a result of our dedication and commitment to Christ, we developed a rigorous discipleship program based largely on the teachings of the Navigators, training and equipping men to impact and transform society for Christ. We conducted this training practically every weekend from 1983 to 1986. At that time I was an active duty Marine and as I was the only married or accompanied Marine with a house, my house became the headquarters and primary meeting place by default. For the next three years, almost every single or unaccompanied Marine that attended our church participated in the training. Throughout the week we kept Scripture memorization cards in our pockets, and when we came together on Fridays and Saturdays we demonstrated what we had learned and memorized. After a time of prayer and instruction we then headed out to the streets of Okinawa, Japan for street witnessing and evangelism. These were some of the most challenging, exciting and rewarding times of my entire Christian walk. Many thanks to our pastor, Bishop Archie Buchanan (now with the Lord) and His lovely wife Hisako for trusting us with this ministry despite our lack of wisdom and experience. I think some of the people in our church thought we were overdoing it, but that did not deter us from our goals of evangelism, street witnessing and making disciples.

The following disciplines formed the foundation of our training:

1. Christ is the center. All Christian training and teaching must be rooted in the revelation of Jesus Christ.

And he is before all things, and in Him all things hold together. He is also the head of the body, the church; and He is the beginning, the first-born from the dead; so that He Himself might come to have first place in everything.
— Colossians 1:17, 18

Jesus must be the essence for all Christian training. All Christian training must reflect Christ's teachings, will, thinking and actions. Jesus is the "exact representation" of the Father (Hebrews 1:3). Our goal as believers and in making disciples is "to become conformed to the image of His Son" (Romans 8:29). During my military career I participated in various high-level exercises and operations. The key to successful operations was the command center. The command center was responsible for communicating the mission's objectives and purpose, providing guidance and direction throughout the duration of operations. Christ is our commander-in-chief and the heart and head of the body, ensuring that the body fulfills its kingdom mandate effectively.

2. The Word of God. The written Word of God (Holy Bible, Old and New Testaments) is our guidebook,

revealing the will and purpose of God for our personal lives and the church.

All Scripture is inspired by God and is profitable for teaching, for reproof, for correction, for training in righteousness; that the man of God may be adequate, equipped for every good work.
— II Timothy 3:16, 17

The infallible Word of God, energized and revealed to us by the Holy Spirit, must become our "daily bread." In the military we had technical manuals (TMs) for every piece of equipment our company or squadron owned and operated. These TMs provided the wealth of knowledge necessary for properly operating, maintaining and repairing our equipment. The TM published the manufacturer's list of authorized repair parts with detailed instructions for troubleshooting and diagnosing any mechanical issues. If there was ever an issue the TM did not address clearly or in the event of questions we were advised to "consult the manufacturer." The believer is no different. The Bible is our "TM" and Jesus is our manufacturer. If ever we feel Scripture does not clearly address a particular issue, we can always pray to the Father for further clarity or resolution.

Again, the importance of reading, studying, meditating on and memorizing Scripture cannot be overstated. The believer must spend time in the Word of God on a consistent basis. The Scriptures will form the basis for the Christian's life and conduct.

3. Prayer. Communication between God and man is accomplished through prayer.

Pray without ceasing.

— I Thessalonians 5:17

Prayer in the life of the believer is paramount. It is through consistent and persistent prayer that we become filled with the presence of Christ. Jesus only ministered after He had spent quality time fellowshipping and communicating with His Father (Matthew 14:23). It is through prayer that we become vulnerable and transparent before God and He responds by filling us with His power (Acts 4:31). Prayer includes waiting silently for God to speak and minister to us, allowing the Holy Spirit to bring Scripture to our remembrance. Singing and rejoicing with thanksgiving can also be incorporated into prayer and praying both in the Holy Spirit and with the understanding is important (I Corinthians 14:15; Ephesians 5:19; 6:18; Jude 20).

4. Witnessing. Sharing our faith in Jesus Christ helps to keep our passion for Christ alive.

"[B]ut you shall receive power when the Holy Spirit has come upon you; and you shall be witnesses both in Jerusalem, and in all Judea and Samaria, and even to the remotest part of the earth."

— Acts 1:8

It is a joy to share our faith in Jesus Christ with others. There are various approaches to witnessing: street witnessing, door to door witnessing, one on one witnessing or personal evangelism and lifestyle witnessing, to name a few. Find the method that best suits your personality and gifting. What is important is that we make the effort to reach others for Christ.

Remember these words of Jesus, "Do you not say, there are yet four months, and then comes the harvest? Behold, I say to you, lift up your eyes, and look on the fields, that they are white for harvest" (John 4:35).

5. Fellowship. Gathering with other believers for encouragement and personal accountability is a necessary component of our faith in Jesus Christ.

And they were continually devoting themselves to the apostles teaching and to fellowship, to the breaking of bread and to prayer.
— Acts 2:42

The benefits of fellowship are innumerable. Fellowship with other believers of like faith protects us from isolation and becoming prey to Satan's devices. Keep in mind that one of the chief tactics of the enemy is to divide and conquer. Christians are strongest when we are united. "And if one can overpower him who is alone, two can resist him. A cord of three strands is not quickly torn apart" (Ecclesiastes 4:12). Scripture reminds us over and over that we are a body and that it is the responsibility of each individual part to encourage and build itself up in love (Ephesians 4:16). Some Christians require more fellowship than others, that's a given. The real issue is that we remain connected to the body of Christ through healthy, life giving, faith building and Christ honoring relationships.

3

FAITH FROM START TO FINISH

"God uses the spoken Word as faith's transportation."　　　　　　　　　　　– Richard Brown III

The Bible teaches that faith is a divine attribute. This simply means that faith comes from God. Genesis chapter one reveals that God spoke all things into existence by His creative Word of Faith, including mankind.

"In the beginning God created the heavens and the earth" (Genesis 1:1).

"And God said, Let there be light; and there was light" (Genesis 1:3).

"Then God said, let us make man in our image, according to our likeness; and let them rule over the fish of the sea and over the birds of the sky and over the cattle and over all the earth" (Genesis 1:26).

Already we see that man has a special relationship to and with God because he was created (male and female) with "god-like" attributes (in the image of God). The question then is, why did God create man to be like Him? God purposed and designed man to exercise dominion and authority in the earth as God's representative and steward. As a consequence of man's assignment, he must possess godly qualities and one such quality is *faith*.

Conversely, animals do not possess faith because it is an attribute of the spirit originating with God, and spirit is one of the distinguishing factors between man and beast. Herein is a clue that man is uniquely designed by God to fulfill destiny and purpose. In the entire universe, only man has the ability to exercise faith in God.

Now that we have established faith's importance as it relates to man and his relationship to God, in that he is created in the image of God, who operates by faith. It is equally important to understand that this faith journey is a marathon not a 100 yard dash. "Faith from start to finish" addresses the need for living faith that seeks to follow, serve and please God on a day-to-day basis. True, a one time act of faith is all that is required to experience the new birth and be declared righteous before God, but keep in mind that salvation is a two-sided coin including both righteousness or justification and sanctification.

The man who lives by his faith in Jesus Christ is declared *righteous* or *justified*. The central theme of the Christian message is, "The righteous shall live by faith" (Romans 1:17). The legal term is *justification* and it is through this justification that we achieve "right standing" with God (Romans 5:1). While justification is an isolated act at the new birth, sanctification is immediate, progressive and final. Sanctification, then, is a process that involves the entire man, spirit, soul and body (I Thessalonians 5:23).

Much like the marathon runner, this type of faith requires prolonged periods of intense physical and mental training as well as strict dieting to reach peak performance and most importantly to finish the race, whereas the sprinter trains for races that only require short bursts of speed and the race is over quickly. It's worth noting that even the build of a marathon runner is strikingly different from a sprinter. Marathoners tend to be lean with very little size or bulk to their muscularity, which is conducive to distance running. Sprinters tend to have large and powerful muscles enabling them to pro-duce quick bursts of speed for relatively short distances.

I believe the writer of Hebrews is referring to a mar-athon runner when he says, "let us also lay aside every encumbrance, and the sin which so easily entangles us, and let us run with endurance the race that is set before us" (Hebrews 12:1).

A believer, if he intends to finish this Christian race must lay aside any encumbrances—any things that, in and of themselves, aren't sin but that might hinder the believer's forward progress in Christ. Certainly any things or conduct that are contrary to the will and Word of God must be put off.

Faith, Fulfillment and Success

Here is where I come into conflict with the consum-er-based gospel, which to me is akin to a trip to your local grocery store or shopping mall where we buy a little of this and a little of that. In other words, picking and choosing only those parts of the gospel we like or agree with, rather than a full, balanced gospel. Case in point, I love sweets, but I know that if I don't eat some carrots, broccoli, green beans, grains, nuts, dairy products, lean meats and proteins, I will hinder my own physical growth and ability to function properly for very long.

The consumer gospel produces consumer Christians. Consumerism is based on supply and demand. Companies, corporations and businesses compete to see who can fill the largest slice of the demand pie. Whichever company can fill the largest slice and generate the largest profits is considered successful. The church isn't much different. The quality and effectiveness of the product does not seem to be of much importance as long as the pastor looks important and successful and the size of the congregation continues to grow. Since we Americans seem to have an obsession with success, we tend to associate ourselves with anything and everything that has the appearance of success.

It is clear to me that God intended for His children to be successful, however, the means by which we achieve that success is important.

Notice God's instructions to Joshua: "This book of the law shall not depart from your mouth, but you shall meditate on it day and night, so that you may be careful to do according to all that is written in it; for then you will make your way prosperous, and then you will have *success*" (Joshua 1:8) (emphasis mine).

The Financial Crisis of 2008 was in large part due to a nation obsessed with the appearance of success.

We bought new houses and cars even though our credit and budgets were already maxed out. Neighbors were competing with neighbors for the biggest house, biggest truck or car, and the banks encouraged us to have it all, now! The church was not to be outdone with our pyramid schemes, prosperity gospel, and special offerings, to include payment for prayers, prophecies and "Christian" paraphernalia.

Hopefully what we've learned from this experience is that God gives fulfillment and success in His time. Stephen Everett calls this the "Zero Factor." There's nothing measureable or otherwise determinable we can do to speed up God's planned purposes.[3] The technological advancements of the 21st century have made instant gratification possible in almost every facet of life. Full-course meals that took the better part of a day to cook and prepare are now prepared in hours or minutes thanks to the microwave oven. Multimillionaires are made instantly due to the lottery. Smartphones put the world at our fingertips, enabling us to communicate globally in seconds due to the advent of the Internet. E-commerce enables ministries to collect tithes and offerings with the swipe of a credit or debit card, eliminating the need to carry large sums of cash or checks.

Have you noticed that God often reveals great potential and promise in the lives of His people only to be followed by seasons of tests, trials, obstacles, detours and delays? Such is the way of those who live by faith (Romans 1:17; II Corinthians 5:7). Remember that no matter how outrageous God's promises may sound, He will make good on His Word (Numbers 23:19; Isaiah 55:8–11).

Often, God allows delays in the fulfillment of His promises to us in order to allow our humanity time to *mature* to the level of our gifts and anointing; I call this "The School of Delayed Fulfillment." Jesus did not enter His earthly ministry until He was thirty, all the while maturing and growing in wisdom: "And Jesus kept increasing in wisdom and stature, and in favor with God and men" (Luke 2:52).

Be assured that when we are submitted to God's timing, our ministries, dreams and visions are in capable hands. Seasons of delayed fulfillment allow the seed that God has sown in us to develop to its full potential, otherwise we may give birth prematurely, which would result in other than ideal consequences. Remember, Abraham had a word from God but grew weary waiting for God to fulfill His promise. As a result of Abraham's impatience, he and Sarah's maid Hagar created Ishmael (Genesis 16:1–16). Ishmael became the Father of the Arab nations, and to this day the sons of Ishmael and the sons of Isaac are in conflict with one another.

As we mature in faith we begin to realize that our success in the kingdom of God is not measured by the size of our house, what we wear, what we drive, the size of our congregations or how many preaching engagements we have. Our success is measured simply by our faith and obedience to God and His Word.

Here is a sampling of how we might measure the growth of the church?

- By how many of our members are following Jesus daily

- By the number of true Christian converts we have won (not the "Christian Exchange Program")
- By healing the sick, casting out devils, raising the dead
- By going to nations and preaching the gospel
- By bringing transformation to cities, regions and nations, advancing the kingdom of God
- By the measure of Christ's gift operating in and through every believer
- By the measure of Christ's character operating in and through every believer
- By the number of true disciples we have made for Christ

As you can see, the list is not exhaustive but addresses some of the more basic commands from God's Word. Our success as believers, as the church, will be measured by our ability to carry out God's Word.

No Spectators Allowed

As leaders, the challenge is to create an environment where people can realize the importance of their participation in the kingdom of God. Our assignment is to help cultivate the seed planted at creation and the new birth. Every Christian, regardless of denomination, gifting, calling, race, gender or anything else should be encouraged to maximize his or her potential in Christ. "God has allotted to each a measure of faith" (Romans 12:3 NASB). This same *measure of faith*, when properly cultivated, has the potential to be a game changer, impacting entire cities, regions or even nations.

It is time for the Western church to return to her first love, exalting the Savior, evangelizing the lost, praying for the sick, expecting miracles and making disciples. The boredom, disappointment and indifference that exist in the body of Christ is largely due to the fact that we have made the kingdom to be about us rather than serving God and humanity. I have found that when a believer has properly identified his or her gifts and calling in Christ and is actively involved in serving God and humanity he does not have time to be bored.

4

FAITH: THE ASSURANCE OF THINGS

"Lord, grant that I may desire more than I can accomplish."[4]

— Michelangelo

I like to use this illustration when I am ministering on the topic of faith. I will ask my audience how many of them checked to ensure the chair they are sitting in is in proper working condition before being seated? Usually the response is no one. Probably our past experience with chairs of this type assured us that the chair would function properly without a thorough inspection of its condition.

Faith in the kingdom of God is no different. True biblical faith is based on *assurance*. God never asks anyone to believe without assurance.

The writer of Hebrews says: "Now faith is the *assurance* of things hoped for, the conviction of things not seen" (Hebrews 11:1) (Italics mine).

So then, faith provides *assurance* and conviction for the things that are not seen. Our human senses like sight, touch and taste enable us to relate to the natural world, while faith connects man to the unseen realm of God. Derek Prince said, "In the Bible, faith is related solely and exclusively to two realities we cannot see with the natural eye: to God and to God's word."[5] This word assurance is the Greek word *hupostasis*, meaning to be placed or to stand under. In general, it means somewhat put under and therefore, used for a basis or foundation.[6] I like to call it "the underlying reality" or "the title deed," proof for our belief in God and His Word. God is faith's assurance. God is absolute assurance.

During the 1990's God put a desire in my heart for a church and ministry training school. When I submitted my paperwork to retire from the Marine Corps and pioneer our ministry in Japan, these were some of the responses I received: Is your wife Japanese? Do you speak Japanese? No one has ever done this before. With little to no experience, Clara and I began to pray and prepare to pioneer the church and school. Needless to say there were many obstacles to overcome with the Japanese government, finances, housing, transportation, school for our youngest daughter, and there were days when it felt like God had abandoned us. All the while I kept rehearsing these Scriptures in my heart, "Now the Lord said to Abram, Go forth from your country, And from your relatives, And from your father's house. To the land which I will show you; And I will make you a great nation, And I will bless you, And make your name great, And so you shall be a blessing" (Genesis 12:1–2). Although I did not have the experience, what I did have was assurance. The word of God became my substance, underlying reality and basis for the fulfillment of God's promises to us. In 1998 we birthed Agape Fellowship Ministries International, Inc., and in 2000, Agape Divinity School (ADS).

I am not advocating that anyone arbitrarily cite Scripture as a means for accomplishing anything for God. I believe there is a key to accomplishing God's will. I had a strong sense, a knowing or conviction in my spirit that the church and school were God's will for us. I believe this strong sense in my spirit was as a result of a personal *rhema,* or word from God, which I will discuss in greater detail later in this book.

No doubt you've heard the phrase "timing is everything." Well, it is one thing to have the assurance of God's Word, but it is equally important to know God's timing. Keep in mind God's timing does not depend upon clocks and calendars. God's timing is based on *kairos. Kairos* means season and time, but not merely a succession of moments, which is *chronos. Kairos* implies that which time gives an opportunity to do. *Kairos,* however, implies not the convenience of the season but the necessity of the task at hand whether the time provides a good, convenient opportunity or not.[7]

Waiting on God

Bill Johnson says, "God is looking for someone who will get out of his or her routine and set up an ambush."[8] Have you ever waited on God? This can be one of the most difficult tests for the man or woman of faith. There is no spiritual gift to assist us in waiting on God. No, waiting on God tests our self-control, which is a fruit of the Spirit and the fruit of the Spirit operates through our character and integrity.

Sadly, too much of our success in life and ministry is measured by how well we *perform*, by what we do. Like Pharisees, we pride ourselves on how much time we spend in prayer, how many Scriptures we've memorized, how much we've given in tithes and offerings and how often we preach or teach. Some time ago I determined that the key to a more successful ministry was early-morning prayer. So I decided that no matter where I was in the world or how busy my itinerary, I would spend an hour in early-morning prayer each day. Most would probably say "that is a noble and wise undertaking." It wasn't long before I noticed a sense of pride developing in my heart because of my "performance" in prayer.

I am learning that it is not what we do for God that makes the greatest impact, but rather what we allow God to do through us, working in conjunction with the Holy Spirit. But working with God often requires seasons of waiting on Him. The fact that we live in a society that is success driven and has grown accustomed to instant gratification makes it increasingly difficult for some to wait patiently on God.

Isaiah says, "Yet those who *wait* for the LORD will gain new strength; They will mount up with wings like eagles, They will run and not get tired, They will walk and not become weary" (Isaiah 40:31) (Italics mine).

It is important to understand here the extended Hebrew meaning of the English word *wait*. Wait—in Hebrew *Qavah*—means to be gathered together, to be joined, to meet, to lie in wait for someone, to expect, to await, to look for patiently, to hope, to be confident and to trust.[9]

The Hebrew definition is not a description of someone waiting idly, without hope, depressed and faithless, but rather with expectation, anticipation and confidence. Waiting on God is a time when God strengthens our faith and resolve for our next assignment in the kingdom. There is a dimension of the anointing of God that God releases upon us only after we have waited patiently on Him.

In 1997 we were informed by our landlord that the Japanese government wanted the land where our church building was located. Immediately Clara and I and the members of our church began to search throughout the island of Okinawa, Japan for a new facility. Months passed and I had become extremely disappointed that we were unable to secure a new location. In my mind I said, "Ok God just let me know when you find the building, I'll be waiting." A few days later, I recall one night about midnight as I was dozing off to sleep, Clara leaned over to me and said, "Richard, God said if you don't go and find the new building the vision is over." I repented for my attitude and got up the next day and went and found the building that we would conduct ministry in for the next thirteen years.

Waiting on God doesn't mean we stop doing what we know to do. It is not a time to quit on God. On the contrary, we continue in a posture of prayer, faith and expectation, knowing that God is preparing to reward our faithfulness in His time.

5

NO RISK, NO RETURN

"If we are holding on too snugly to our stuff, make no mistake about it: God pursues us through the medium of the cross to let it go."[10]

— Stephen Everett

Many times during our assignment in Japan as missionaries, I can recall feeling as if I was walking a tightrope in a circus act, without a safety net. Perhaps you have felt this way also. I wish I could tell you that Clara and I spoke or read Japanese when we decided to retire from the Marine Corps and pioneer a ministry in Okinawa, Japan; we didn't. I would like to tell you that we had major support from churches and organizations in the U.S.; we didn't. But, much like an investment banker, we gambled that the reward would far exceed our initial investment; it did. We discovered for ourselves that God can use mustard seed faith (Matthew 17:20).

There were many highs and lows during our assignment in Japan. Leading our first Japanese husband and wife to Jesus was among the highs, as well as sending our first Japanese pastor Ichiro Kuba to pioneer his church. One of the hardest challenges we faced was watching so many of the American believers we had grown to love be reassigned to new bases throughout the U.S. and the world. Our ministry was like a revolving door. People would come in to be trained and go out to serve. Another major difficulty after the Financial Crisis of 2008 was watching the Japanese Yen rate drop to 74 Yen to the U.S. Dollar. With the dollar value dropping essentially to 74 cents, our ability to fund missions and ministry was drastically impacted. However, we experienced God's grace through numerous financial miracles, from finding cash in our mailbox to receiving phone calls from believers whose hearts God had touched to make large donations to the ministry just in time to pay the bills.

From one simple investment in the kingdom of God souls have been saved, healed, delivered and encouraged from Japan to Singapore, and churches and ministries have been pioneered from Albany, Georgia to Phoenix, Arizona. Some of the lives we've touched, transformed and trained over the years are no longer in touch with us, but to God be all the glory!

During 2009, I had been preaching and teaching two messages: 1) No risk, No Return and 2) Launch Out into the Deep. I ministered this message from Japan to the U.S. and from the U.S. to South Korea, Singapore and Australia.

One Saturday afternoon in November of 2010, Clara had been upstairs praying, and the Holy Spirit impressed upon her heart these words, "launch out into the deep." At the conclusion of Clara's prayer time she came downstairs and said to me, "Richard do the words 'launch out into the deep' mean anything to you?" I replied, "No." Later, after pondering on those words for a moment, the Holy Spirit brought back to my remembrance how I had been preaching those words everywhere for practically an entire year and now those words were coming home to roost.

Soon I began to receive a series of phone calls with offers to relocate our ministry to a much better location. While the financial obligation where we were located at the time was manageable, and the facility was very nice, the new location presented a fresh challenge, exciting opportunities and a much-needed change of scenery. I took a couple of months to weigh the pros and cons and to pray and seek the will of God. Finally, I came to the conclusion that we should make the investment in the new location. Of course, I realized this was not a decision I should make on my own so I consulted with Clara and she supported my decision. After gaining Clara's agreement, I then approached our leaders with the proposed move where I met with some resistance. As I mention later in the book, unfortunately, vision often causes separation.

Abraham couldn't fulfill vision and take his nephew lot with him (Genesis 13:14–18). Joseph shared his dream with his father and brothers and his brothers plotted to kill him, thus he was sold into slavery (Genesis 37:18–36). Jesus informed His disciples that He was about to be crucified and Peter tried to rebuke him (Mark 8:31–33).

One of my leaders, intimately familiar with our church finances, requested a meeting with me after church, recognizing that this relocation would require a substantial financial commitment on our part voiced her concerns. During this meeting I was informed that financially we were in no position to relocate and she tendered her resignation from our ministry. To say the least, Clara and I were disappointed, surprised and devastated. No sooner than I began to "step out in faith" did the resistance begin to mount. Often, when a miracle is needed, God will put a demand on your faith, finances and resources. Case in point, Peter and his associates had been fishing all night long and caught nothing when Jesus arrived on the scene and requested to use Peter's boat as a teaching platform (Luke 5:3). At the conclusion of His teaching, Jesus instructed Peter to "launch out into the deep" and let down his nets for a catch (Luke 5:4). I can imagine Peter must have been exhausted and discouraged after fishing all night and catching nothing. However, something supernatural happened here. Peter received the instructions from Jesus as a *rhema*—a faith producing, power-filled, word from God (Luke 5:5).[11] Peter released his faith upon the Word spoken to him from God. So great was the catch of fish Peter caught that day that he had to summon his friends to help bring them ashore (Luke 5:7). So profound was the miracle Peter received from the Lord that day that he and his friends dropped everything and followed Jesus (Luke 5:8–11). Peter risked it all that day and as a result countless multitudes have been inspired by his faith and obedience.

As difficult as it was, we relocated our ministry, which enabled us to continue our presence in Asia for another three years. Souls were saved, healings took place and lives were transformed as a result of the risk taken. Not only did we continue to minister the gospel in Japan and continue to train leaders, but it was also during this time that God expanded our influence into Indonesia and Hong Kong, China.

What do you possess that God can use to produce your miracle? Remember, God will never require from you what He has not already given you!

6

THE MEASURE OF FAITH – PLACE AND FUNCTION

"It is easier to say that we are significant, instead of saying I am significant. Yet it is the discovery of this truth that liberates us into true humility."[12]
– Bill Johnson

As I made my transition from twenty four years of ministry in Okinawa, Japan as senior pastor to five-fold ministry gift to the body of Christ, I became, once again, keenly aware of the importance of *place* and *function* to the believer and the kingdom of God.

The Sixth Man

Consider for a moment a professional basketball team. The National Basketball Association (NBA) has what is known as a "sixth man." This sixth man is vital to the team's ability to reach and succeed at the championship level. The sixth man is not one of the five starters, but must possess the same level of skill and ability as a starter, as he will come off the bench to give his team a spark during the game. Usually, the sixth man will possess exceptional scoring, defensive or rebounding skills. One such sixth man is Manu Ginobili of the San Antonio Spurs. During his team's recent championship run, Ginobili was instrumental in providing an offensive spark off the bench, catapulting his team to yet another NBA Championship.

Now, keep in mind the sixth man concept. The sixth man is submitted to his coach and the needs and goals of his team. Although highly talented and gifted, he is willing to come off the bench when his abilities are needed. The sixth man could easily be a star player on another team, but on this particular team he has accepted the role of sixth man. In a similar manner, the believer is willing to use his gift when and where he is needed at the discretion of the coach.

For the purpose of clarity the "coach" could very well be the pastor, bishop, minister, department head or even God. It is imperative that we, the sixth man, recognize and submit to God-ordained leadership as we settle into our place and function for the season we are in.

The body of Christ operates much the same as a professional basketball team. Each member of the body of Christ is gifted but must be willing to accept his or her role, place and function, enabling the body to accomplish its God-given assignment in the earth.

Apostle Paul recognized the importance of place and function: "For by the grace given to me I say to everyone among you not to think of himself more highly than he ought to think, but to think with sober judgment, each according to *the measure of faith* that God has assigned" (Romans 12:3 ESV) (Italics mine).

The grace Paul is referring to here is not saving grace. This grace incorporates the broader definition of the Greek word *charis* (Strong's #5485), meaning a divine endowment, thus enabling every believer to become an asset and provide some benefit or bounty to the body of Christ. The measure, or Greek *metron* (Strong's #3358), is determined by Christ.

Every believer has been assigned a measure of faith. The measure of faith is that faith which God has allotted to a specific individual for his or her place and function in the body of Christ.

For example:
Place—Where do you fit in the body of Christ? Are you an arm, leg or an eye? Are you senior leadership, laity, department head, director or worker (Romans 12:4–8)?

Function—Are you called to the five-fold ministry of apostle, prophet, evangelist, pastor or teacher; do you prophesy, teach, show mercy, operate the gifts of faith, miracles, tongues, gifts of healing (I Corinthians 12:4–11; Ephesians 4:7, 11, 12)?

Requisite to finding our place and function in the body of Christ is our personal devotion and submission to God daily. In Romans chapter 12, Paul borrows from Old Testament examples of the priesthood. Apostle Paul urges, "present your bodies a living and holy sacrifice, acceptable to God, which is your spiritual service of worship" (Romans 12:1). Sacrifice, submission and worship are distinctly priestly functions. Under the Old Covenant the priests followed a daily ritual of strict washings, animal sacrifices and sprinkling of blood. With the advent of the New Covenant in and through Christ's blood, every believer is considered a priest and lives a life wholly and completely dedicated to God daily (I Peter 2:5, 9).

Romans 12:2 underscores the importance of transformation through a renewed mind. As the believer's thought life is transformed on a consistent basis, he finds his place and function in the body of Christ, thus accepting God's good, acceptable and perfect will for his life and ministry. Religion focuses on rules and requirements to govern the external conduct such as attire, food and entertainment; this is not God's focus here. Inner change and transformation is the goal, a renewed mind, new attitudes, values and priorities are the goal.

The key then, to identifying our place and function is a revelation from God. Paul said this: "Because the mind set on the flesh is hostile toward God; for it does not subject itself to the law of God, for it is not even able to do so" (Romans 8:7).

God reveals Himself to man's *renewed* intellect. Consider again, for a moment, that carnal man's mind is the enemy of God. No soldier would ever reveal his secrets or strategies to an enemy, someone who is hostile toward him. This same principle applies to God and could explain why we sometimes find it difficult to understand the things of God.

One of the challenges I faced in my senior pastor role in Japan was how to incorporate five-fold ministry gifts, transferring from local churches in the U.S. into our local assembly. I found that there can be vast differences in requirements and expectations for ordination from church to church and from denomination to denomination. Often, when one has served as pastor or senior leadership in one assembly, the expectation is that they will assume the same or a similar position or function in the new ministry.

Here again, it is imperative that we enter into prayer and submission to God's will and direction. The Holy Spirit will lead us into our place and function based on His purpose and design and not ours.

Case in point, in 1987 my family and I transferred from Okinawa, Japan where I had served as senior pastor of a local church to California. As Clara and I sought God in prayer, we did not sense that it was God's will for us to pastor in California. As a matter of fact, I was asked to consider a pastoral position by two different church bodies. Eventually, I found my place in the adult Sunday school department as a teacher and an associate minister on the pastor's staff. As I settled into my new place and function I found the greatest satisfaction and fulfillment. I watched as the attendance, level of expectation and faith grew to new heights. The assignment in California became one of my most rewarding and satisfying assignments in the kingdom of God.

Your function as a five-fold ministry gift is irrevocable (Romans 11:29). Place, however, is largely dependent upon the need in the local body and placement by the Holy Spirit into a particular assembly of believers.

A believer's place and function may vary from one local body to another as in the case of Philip. In the Jerusalem church, Philip functioned as a deacon, but when he traveled he did the work of an evangelist (Acts 6:5; 8:26-40).

Often, during the time that I served as senior pastor in Japan, I traveled to various Asian nations for ministry. Whenever I traveled, Clara, an evangelist by calling, would assume the pastoral duties and responsibilities of our church. It was always sort of amusing to me that upon my return, at the soonest possible opportunity, Clara would notify me that she was releasing the mantle of pastoral responsibility back to me.

My wife, Clara, is one of the best examples I know of for understanding the measure of faith and place and function in the body of Christ. I have shared this story many times to congregations throughout Asia and the U.S. Often when Clara and I travel together and I am able financially, I will use our frequent flyer miles and upgrade our seats to business class. Those of you who have traveled on long international flights know that the seat and the amenities can make all the difference on these flights. Well, no sooner than we reach cruising altitude (usually, 35,000 or 38,000 feet) Clara is out of her seat positioning herself near the flight attendants' area and restrooms in an attempt to engage someone, anyone in a conversation about Jesus Christ. She often spends long periods of time witnessing and sharing Christ with anyone who will listen. Occasionally she will return to her seat to inform me that she has led someone to Christ and to introduce them to me.

A couple of years ago, Clara and I were traveling to our History Maker International conference in Taipei, Taiwan. At the time we were living in Okinawa, Japan, which is only a fifty-minute flight from Taiwan. Because I booked our flight using frequent flyer miles, we had to fly from Okinawa, to Seoul, South Korea and from Seoul to Taiwan. Clara was not too thrilled about this because she actually does not enjoy flying. As usual, after reaching cruising altitude, Clara made her way to the flight attendants' station where she began to witness to a Korean flight attendant. About an hour and a half into the flight, Clara and the flight attendant approached my seat and Clara informed me that she had just led this young lady to Christ. Clara's consolation prize for taking this out of the way flight was that she got to win a soul to Christ.

After more than thirty years of ministry, I am both humbled and amazed at how God uses the measure of faith He deposited into Clara's life to minister the good news of the gospel of Christ to hurting and lost souls. I believe the ministry of the evangelist is so effective in her life in part because she has submitted to the Holy Spirit's placement in the body and to her function as an evangelist. I have learned that ministries and gifts are most effective when we are settled into the Holy Spirit's determined place and function in the kingdom of God.

How to Identify Your Measure of Faith

This may sound like a simple task, but there are important steps and principles to consider in this process.

1. Are you born again (John 3:1–3)? It is imperative that those who represent God and His ministries are genuinely saved.

2. Can you attest to a clear call of God upon your life (Ephesians 4:11)? There should be a clear knowing within the heart of a believer that he or she is called by God. The call can come through various means: God's audible voice, a dream, a vision, a prophetic word or by the witness of the Holy Spirit within the believer's heart.

3. Has the pastor or leadership where you fellowship recognized God's call upon your life (Acts 6:6; 13:3; Titus 1:5)? One of church leadership's responsibilities is to help believer's identify and confirm the genuine call of God upon their lives. This should be accomplished through those to whom we have submitted our lives for accountability and who can attest to our character, conduct and function in the local body of Christ. Licensing, ordination or official recognition of ministry is best served by those who witness our lives on a consistent basis. Or if recognition is coming through a denomination or organization, the individual who is being recognized should have the support and agreement of the local pastor.

4. Pray and ask God to reveal His purpose to you. Through our communion and fellowship with God, much can be revealed and accomplished (Jeremiah 33:3; Matthew 7:7, 8; Philippians 4:6).

5. Ask those you have ministered to to testify to the affects of your ministry and gifts upon their lives. Often you will hear a common theme in the comments of those you minister to. For example, many times I've been told that my teaching, preaching or ministry brought clarity, understanding and encouragement to the listener. This information has aided me in developing the teaching ministry imparted to me through the measure of faith.

6. This will reemphasize number 3, but allow senior leaders to affirm your gifts and calling. Generally this is accomplished through those with more wisdom and experience than peer level leaders and associates.

7. Search the Scriptures for confirmation and Biblical examples. Read books written by proven Christian authors in the field or ministry that you function in.

This list was not intended to be exhaustive, but can be used as a general guideline for identifying gifts and callings.

A Melting Pot

As a child, I enjoyed watching my mother prepare meals. Of course watching her prepare meals also came with privileges. I got to taste whatever she was cooking. One of my favorite meals was spaghetti. I would watch intently as my mother sliced and diced green peppers, onions and celery. After browning a pound or two of ground beef, she would sauté the vegetables and then mix these ingredients into a pot of tomato sauce. She then added spices such as salt, pepper, garlic, oregano and parmesan cheese. Once all of the ingredients were mixed into the sauce, she would allow the sauce to simmer. Pour the sauce over a plate of spaghetti noodles, add garlic bread and enjoy.

In many ways the body of Christ resembles a melting pot, and the measure of faith is God's way of ensuring that all of the necessary ingredients have been prepared. God, having bestowed gifts and faith upon every believer ensures there is a healthy balance in the church and kingdom.

Apostle Paul uses a slightly different analogy to emphasize the same point: "For the body is not one member, but many. If the foot should say, 'Because I am not a hand, I am not a part of the body.' It is not for this reason any the less a part of the body" (I Corinthians 12:14- 15).

Paul instructs the Corinthian church on the importance of each believer's place and function within the corporate expression. The church would do well to accept and embrace the diversity of gifts, ministries, talents and abilities dispersed throughout God's Kingdom.

It is a misuse of precious time to debate the relevance of gifts and ministries God has placed in His body. While we all may lean toward or prefer specific gifts, all are necessary at the appropriate time and in their appropriate place. The point is this, every believer and every gift and ministry adds value to every believer in the body of Christ.

Paul's words to the church in Ephesus: "From whom the whole body, being fitted and held together by that which every joint supplies, according to the proper working of each individual part, causes the growth of the body for the building up of itself in love" (Ephesians 4:16).

It is likely we will never achieve the level of success and effectiveness we desire while pursuing the ministry of our choosing, but as we learn to surrender to God daily through the renewing of our minds (Romans 12:1–2), we will enter that measure of faith and anointing that releases purpose and fulfillment in our lives.

7

UNDERSTANDING YOUR SPHERE OF AUTHORITY

"I'm a man under orders; I also give orders. I tell one soldier, 'Go,' and he goes; another, 'Come,' and he comes; my slave, 'Do this,' and he does it."
— Luke 7:8 THE MESSAGE

My mother had a saying she used whenever we kids were being too bossy with one another. She would say, "who died and left you boss?" This was my mom's way of letting us know that as long as we were living under her roof, she was still in charge. Regardless of our age or seniority among the siblings, our use of authority at 3564 Brighton Road was subject to and at the discretion of Eunice Brown.

God designed His kingdom to operate much the same way. It says something about a man's integrity when he refuses to take credit for something he had no personal investment in.

Paul said, "Thus my ambition has been to preach the Gospel, not where Christ's name has already been known, lest I build on another man's foundation" (Romans 15:20 AMP).

The Book of Acts chronicles Paul and Barnabas' missionary journeys into Asia Minor and Europe. These mighty apostles were not interested in preaching where other men preached, but desired to pioneer new churches and develop strong Christian leadership in new territories. As the brethren prayed and fasted in Antioch, the Holy Spirit directed Barnabas and Saul to be sent to the mission field (Acts 13:1–3). As a result of these men's faith and obedience, they experienced much fruit from their labors.

I'm not sure why or even how to explain it, but from my earliest years in ministry, I can recall having a desire to minister, teach and preach in foreign lands. As a local pastor in Okinawa, Japan, I dreamed of one day reaching beyond the Americans and Japanese in my congregation. This passion of mine to reach all kinds of people led me to Colorado Springs, Colorado. Here, while attending our annual Apostolic Council for Educational Accountability Conference (ACEA), I met Richard William. Not only did Richard and I share the same first name, but we also shared a passion for training young people, discipleship and bringing trans- formation and revival to the nations. We each had pio- neered ministry training schools and were eager to see our students impacting the kingdom of God.

Richard and Debbie William pioneered History Maker International, Singapore, and soon after invited me to join them as an advisor. At its peak the network included pastors, Christian leaders, business leaders and youth from the following nations: Singapore, Japan, China, South Korea, Russia, South Africa, Malaysia, Indonesia, Sri Lanka, India, Nepal, Mongolia, Pakistan, Australia, Taiwan, Myanmar and the United States. Soon I found myself ministering in many of these nations. On occasion Richard has asked me to minister in his stead. The Holy Spirit had expanded my "sphere" of authority through my relationship with Richard William.

While many of my ministry colleagues' and friends' primary emphasis has been in the U.S., my sphere of influence and authority has been primarily in Asia. I've learned that a man's most effective ministry will be to those to whom he has been sent. It is important to have a sense of the measure of grace upon one's life and ministry for God's people. Paul was an apostle to the Gentiles, while Peter was sent to the Jews.

Notice what Paul says here:

But on the contrary, seeing that I had been entrusted with the gospel to the uncircumcised, just as Peter had been to the circumcised (for He who effectually worked for Peter in his apostleship to the circumcised effectually worked for me also to the Gentiles).   – Galatians 2:7, 8

Paul recognized that his measure of faith and apostleship was "tailor made" for ministry to the Gentiles. Although we may possess a genuine calling and anointing as apostles, bishops or pastors from the Lord, that does not necessarily make us an apostle or bishop to everyone in the body of Christ.

Paul said this in his letter to the Corinthians: "But we will not boast beyond our measure, but within the measure of the *sphere* which God apportioned to us as a measure, to reach even as far as you" (II Corinthians 10:13) (emphasis added).

And again Paul says: "not boasting beyond our measure, that is, in other men's labors, but with the hope that as your faith grows, we shall be, within our *sphere*, enlarged even more by you" (II Corinthians 10:15) (emphasis added).

Throughout Paul's ministry, he was careful not to take credit for another man's work. I believe this is an important lesson for Christian leaders in the season we are currently in. We must resist the tendency to measure the worth of our ministries based upon numbers alone. This ill in the body of Christ often leads to disunity and division within the kingdom of God. Some men, because of insecurity, are willing to take shortcuts, recruiting men and women like unrestricted free agents in the sports market to join their ministry team. Often current membership or ministry affiliations are disregarded, and gifted men and women are added to the ministry team in an effort to increase numbers, financial gain or ministry status. I call this the "Christian Exchange Program." Not that the people of God belong to a pastor or Christian leader, on the contrary, the people belong to God and we are stewards or under-shepherds for our Lord and Savior Jesus Christ, but as leaders we must at all costs display a higher level of integrity to the people of God.

After all, Jesus did not call us to build personal empires, but rather to expand and increase the kingdom of Almighty God! The kingdom of God grows by means of the new birth, pioneering new ministries and opening up new regions and territories to the gospel. Pioneering new ministries and churches takes time. Apostle Paul remained in Ephesus for two years teaching, preaching and training the disciples daily in the school of Tyrannus. As a result of Paul's commitment and sacrifice, "all who lived in Asia heard the word of the Lord, both Jews and Greeks" (Acts 19:10). In a world where no one waits for anything anymore, where high-speed Internet isn't fast enough, fast food isn't fast enough and technology puts the world at our fingertips, it is no wonder the church is in such a hurry. Paul demonstrates to us in the Book of Acts that it takes time to build quality leaders and strong churches.

Recently, Clara and I relocated to Clara's home-town of Jacksonville, North Carolina, where our children and grandchildren reside. It has been a tremendous learning curve for us to attend a church where we are not the senior pastors. We currently attend Agape, Christians in Action Church, under the pastoral leadership of Kenneth and Angela Lester. Kenney and Angie are former members of Agape Fellowship Japan and graduates of Agape Divinity School. After a prescribed and deliberate time of teaching and training, these two were sent to Jacksonville to pioneer a new church. Clara and I have no authority in Agape CIA other than that we function as the spiritual "grandparents" of the church. While I provide "apostolic covering" to Kenney and Angie, we submit to their pastoral authority. It is both refreshing and humbling to see what God is doing through this couple.

With this new assignment comes the challenge of discerning my new function and place. Here, my primary emphasis will be to transform men from sainthood to sonship. One of the fundamentals of apostolic ministry is to propel men from blessing and promise into destiny, purpose and fulfillment as mature sons in the kingdom of God.

8

BRINGING YOUR FAITH TO MATURITY

"It is one thing to play with dolls or someone else's baby and another thing to give birth to your own child."   – Richard Brown

L ike most children, my brothers, sisters and I would sometimes get into mischief or perhaps conduct that our parents did not approve of. Whenever my oldest sister, Vanessa, was around she would say, "I'm telling on you." She did this so frequently that often my mother's response was, "worry about yourself and you'll have your hands full." In other words, "just make sure you are doing what I told you to do and I'll take care of the rest."

The body of Christ is no different. We sometimes get into things that are cause for debate and arguments. As we all develop and mature in our gifts, callings and faith we will focus less on theological debates and arguments and more on accomplishing our God ordained assignments. Christians debate such things as; what is the proper baptism formula, are tongues for today, the relevance of five-fold ministry for today, can women be ordained, is denominationalism of God and what constitutes "Christian" music. All of these topics and more are worthy of our attention, but the body of Christ must be careful not to major on minors.

After the crucifixion, death, burial and resurrection of Jesus, Peter attempted to return to his former occupation, fisherman (John 21:3). Jesus, knowing Peter's weaknesses knew exactly where to find Peter and the other disciples—by the sea. After fishing all night long, Peter and the disciples caught nothing. Once again, Jesus appeared to His disciples and provided a miraculous catch of fish (John 21:6).

As Peter and the disciples dined, Jesus spoke these words to Peter:

> "Simon, son of John, do you love Me more than these?" He said to Him, Yes, Lord; You know that I love you. He said to him, Tend My lambs.
> — John 21:15

Herein lies one of the fundamental keys to our success in the kingdom of God; release your measure of faith to accomplish what Jesus commanded you to do. This is a sign of maturity. Jesus commanded Peter to feed his lambs (John 21:15 KJV). Immediately following Jesus' command to Peter, he asks, "Lord, and what about this man" (John 21:21)? Unfortunately, the typical human response to God's commands is to question and debate the instructions. The primary issue is; what are God's instructions to us?

Your assignment will likely differ from others in the kingdom, but kingdom assignments will often overlap and have similarities. Your specific assignment and corresponding measure of faith will be uniquely tailored to you. This is not to say that we should not value one another's gifts and callings. On the contrary, God distributes varying degrees or measures of faith and gifting to each individual believer. This also lends itself to maximum participation and cooperation within the corporate body.

Paul reminds us:

And since we have gifts that differ according to the grace given to us, let us each exercise them accordingly: if prophecy, according to the proportion of his faith.   – Romans 12:6

When we attempt to rank gifts and callings by human standards, our lack of understanding and immaturity is revealed. As a general rule, when I teach on the subject of gifts and callings, I teach that we should desire that the best gifts of the Holy Spirit be in operation in a given service or setting. What or who determines this; the Holy Spirit Himself. Here is, perhaps, a simplified example: If a physically ill person enters a particular service and a believer who operates in the gifts of healing ministers healing to this person, then the best gift at that particular time might have been the gifts of healing. I'm pretty sure the person on the receiving end of the healing would agree. Similarly, if there are sinners present and the evangelist ministers the gospel to the point that men repent of their sins and are converted, then the five-fold ministry gift of the evangelist was likely the best gift at that time. In every instance the gifts that produce the results that accomplish God's will and bring glory and honor to Him are the best gifts.

During Jesus' encounter with the woman at the well, she attempted to cloud the issue by engaging Jesus in a theological debate regarding the proper place of worship. Jesus countered this woman's argument by informing her that worship is no longer regulated to a particular time or place, but is a matter of worshipping in spirit, reality, honesty and integrity (John 4:1–24). As a result of her encounter with Jesus this Samaritan woman received faith, and with her testimony evangelized many from her city (John 4:39–42).

As I mature, both as a man and a five-fold ministry gift to the body of Christ, I am seeing with greater spiritual perception the Father's desire for every believer to realize his or her potential in Christ. It is with this knowledge of the Father's desire that I have attempted to disciple, train and mentor men and women for Christ. Over the years I have been blessed to bring gifted young men along with me on ministry trips both in the U.S. and Asia. I recall one such trip to South Korea where I was invited to be the keynote speaker for a summer camp meeting. The participants of this particular meeting were various South Korean church leaders and their congregations. On the second night of the meetings following the ministry of the Word, I began conducting altar ministry with the laying on of hands, prayer and prophecy. There were nearly one thousand people to pray for and minister to that evening. As I was ministering, my armorbearer, Jaime, was called away by the crowd, and before long I looked up from praying and saw Jaime praying and ministering to the people in another prayer line across the auditorium. Like Jesus' disciples, Jaime was practicing what he had seen me do numerous times. I knew that he was ready because we spent our days in prayer, the Word and ministering to the Lord. This particular evening Jaime gained valuable ministry experience that will follow him for the rest of his life.

I think one of the most exciting and promising Scriptures in the entire Bible is found in II Corinthians 3:18, which reads, "But we all, with unveiled face beholding as in a mirror the glory of the Lord, are being transformed into the same image from glory to glory, just as from the Lord, the Spirit." The idea here is that we become what we behold. As we consistently fellowship and commune with Jesus, the Holy Spirit transforms us into the very same image. And the more we are transformed into the image of Christ the more we are able to live as He lived and do what He did.

Through the new birth we have received salvation and the seed of Christ-like character. Through the measure of faith the Father has distributed to us various Christ-like gifts, abilities and ministries. Father God gave gifts to men not so that we could stand in awe of one another, but so that we could minister God's love and grace to the lost and dying humanity around us. As a result of our gifts and ministries, men give honor and glory to God.

Jesus said this in the beatitudes: "Give, and it will be given to you; good measure, pressed down, shaken together, running over, they will pour into your lap. For by your standard of measure it will be measured to you in return" (Luke 6:38).

No, I am not preparing to receive an offering! Although this Scripture is often read preceding the offering in many churches, I believe we have missed the larger meaning. In our attempts to fill the offering baskets, we have neglected to apply this Scripture to giving of ourselves, our gifts, our possessions. Whatever we give, we will receive in like measure. Showing mercy, grace, love and forgiveness all comes back to us in proportion to the measure we have shown to others. I believe this to be a much-overlooked principle of God's Word. Prior to sending His disciples out to conduct ministry, Jesus said these words, "Heal the sick, raise the dead, cleanse the lepers, cast out demons; freely you received, freely give" (Matthew 10:8). Essentially, Jesus was saying just do what you have seen me do.

In 2009, I was blessed to take two young men from my congregation in Japan with me on a ministry trip to Australia. I was invited as one of the keynote speakers for a History Maker Youth Conference. During the day and evening sessions, Tim and German received the Word and impartation released through the speakers. By night, Tim and German formed a team from the youth attending the conference and evangelized the streets of the area near the conference. Each morning, with great enthusiasm they would brief me on the results of their street evangelism the previous evening. These brothers simply put the training they received while attending our church in Japan to work in Australia. Today they are serving their communities as an assistant pastor and a law enforcement officer.

In 2013, Fred and Tywan accompanied me to Hong Kong for a History Maker Conference where we were blessed to share the gospel, witness to and pray for many of our Chinese brothers and sisters in Christ. The highlight of these meetings was the opportunity to minister salvation to a group of Chinese who had traveled from mainland China to attend the meetings. Likewise, these young men saw their faith stretched as they assisted me in ministering to these hungry souls. It is priceless opportunities such as these that allow those we are training to release their measure of faith. These opportunities become building blocks for growth and maturity. As Christian leaders we must capitalize on every contingency to encourage and recognize the measure of faith operating through others. Barnabas was one who understood the importance of recognizing the gifts and abilities of others.

> And he left for Tarsus to look for Saul; and when he had found him, he brought him to Antioch. And it came about that for an entire year they met with the church, and taught considerable numbers; and the disciples were first called Christians in Antioch.   – Acts 11:25, 26

Barnabas and Saul or Paul, became one of the most "dynamic duos" of the entire Bible. What is often over-looked regarding this relationship is the fact that it was not long before Paul assumed the lead role in their missionary endeavors. As we draw nearer to the return of our Lord and Christ, I believe we will begin to see more examples such as this. Mature leaders will begin to release the reigns of leadership and pass the baton to those we have trained and like Barnabas and Paul, our trainees will far exceed our accomplishments, bringing glory and honor to our God and Father.

If the 21st century church is to do its part in fulfilling the Great Commission, then we must not only educate up and coming leaders, but also provide them with opportunities to give away what they have received from the Lord. The glory that is released into our lives as we commune with and encounter the Lord was meant to be released into the lives of people everywhere. The same anointing and glory that rests upon our lives after we have consecrated and prepared ourselves to preach, teach or minister God's Word should rest upon us when we make a trip to WalMart, Starbucks or McDonalds. This anointing rests upon us in our homes, workplaces and schools.

Over the years I have witnessed various men and women of God who were genuinely gifted and anointed of God fall short of their intended goals due to a lack of spiritual maturity. Some because of what I would call an "orphan spirit" or insecurities. It is time for leaders to "seize the day," look beyond their faults and short-comings and harvest these "diamonds in the rough." It is time to see our Timothys and Tituses, Deborahs and Esthers reach their full potential in Christ.

9

REALIZING THE POTENTIAL OF YOUR SEED

"Abraham was first named 'father' and then became a father because he dared to trust God to do what only God could do: raise the dead to life, with a word make something out of nothing."
— Romans 4:17 THE MESSAGE

There are many similarities between nature and the kingdom of God. Some of the most profound teaching in all of Scripture can be found in Jesus' teaching on "The Parable of the Sower" in Matthew chapter 13 and Mark chapter 4. This teaching reminds me of one of my earliest science projects in grade school. Each student was instructed to bring an empty milk carton to class along with a few flower seeds. The carton was cut in half and filled with dirt or soil. I then placed a few seeds into the soil and placed my carton along with my classmate's cartons on the windowsill in our classroom where they would be exposed to the sunlight. Each day we would add a little water to our cartons and to our amazement, after several days a plant began to sprout up out of the soil. As we continued to care for and nurture these plants they grew into beautiful flowers.

Throughout this book I have been emphasizing that God has apportioned to every man "The Measure of Faith." As encouraging as this information is, it is imperative that we understand that this faith is imparted in seed form. What God gives or imparts to us is *potential*. In the kingdom of God, potential is determined by the *nature of the seed*. Nature is a clue to purpose. This is powerful because Scripture reveals that whatever is a result of God's seed or nature overcomes the world (I John 5:4).

Seed contains an *embryo*, an organism that enables it to reproduce after its kind. It contains a nature, in this case God's nature, "a divine nature" (II Peter 1:4). The word nature comes from the Greek—*phusis*, meaning growth by germination or expansion; that which is a result of God's natural production.[13] God imparts faith, gifts, ministries, callings and abilities in seed form.

The Gospel of Mark reveals some very startling facts:

"The kingdom of God is like a man who casts seed upon the soil; and goes to bed at night and gets up by day, and the seed sprouts up and grows—how, he himself does not know. The soil produces crops by itself..."
— Mark 4:26-28

What then? It is the believer's responsibility to live by faith, and God is responsible for producing results. The Holy Spirit is watching over our seed while we are asleep, to cause it to grow, increase and mature. God told Jeremiah, "I am watching over My word to perform it" (Jeremiah 1:12). The measure of faith that God has given to an individual believer will operate with little effort. So encouraged, motivated and inspired are you when you operate your measure of faith that if someone wakes you up at two in the morning, you are ready to minister your gift. This is how you know it is a gift from God; you simply release your faith and God gives the increase.

I'm convinced that God intended for His seed to multiply both naturally and spiritually (Genesis 1:26–28). From a natural and biological standpoint, in order to reproduce the highest level of intimacy between a man and a woman is necessary; there must be a pregnancy. The same is necessary spiritually. God's people must be impregnated with or by God's Word and Spirit, which requires a deliberate plan, fellowship and intimacy.

Visualize Your Dream

Equally important to the potential of the seed is *vision*. An effective leader will possess the ability to create an atmosphere conducive for the seed to grow; this requires vision. Vision is the ability to create a desired future; it does not focus on what is, but rather on what could be. Jesus said, "What things soever ye desire, when ye pray, believe that ye receive them, and ye shall have them" (Mark 11:24 KJV). The key here is to pray the answer not the problem, what you desire not what you have. The flesh and emotions will attempt to focus on the problem; this is detrimental to faith because you produce whatever you visualize the most. For example, TV commercials constantly bombard our minds until finally we find ourselves buying products that we don't necessarily need. Focusing on the negative only produces more of the negative. The believer must realize that the negative is not his vision.

So important is vision that Proverbs says, "Where there is no vision, the people perish" (Proverbs 29:18 KJV). One of the greatest challenges to experiencing great vision in the kingdom of God is *mediocrity*. Mediocrity is a dream and vision killer. Too often the church settles for "good enough" because we have not been exposed to excellence. I have discovered that a man is destined to reproduce at the level he has been exposed to. This is why it is important to get out of our familiar surroundings and comfort zones and see something new or different that will challenge our mind and spirit. During the mid 1990's Clara and I would travel from Japan annually to one of the largest ministries in the Pacific Northwest to expose ourselves to teaching and ministry that would stretch our faith. Exposure to this ministry allowed us to see what could be not what is. Subsequently, we began to travel to Los Angeles where my spiritual father and friend, Bishop Virgil D. Patterson, Sr., taught us to pray and confess the Word of God.

As you become a visionary leader, understand that God is going to enlarge and strengthen your imagination, abilities and mental playing field, enabling you to think big in small places. During the time that Clara and I were pioneering our church, ministry training school and ministry in Japan and Asia, I learned that I could not think of the thing that God could not do through me. God is able to do above and beyond what we can think or imagine (Ephesians 3:20).

When real vision takes hold it will begin to separate you from those whose only desire is to maintain the status quo. Vision will cause some people to become so uncomfortable that they will have to separate themselves from you, but you will gain others who are in search of real vision. It wasn't until Lot separated himself from Abram that God began to reveal His vision and promise to Abram. You cannot fulfill vision and take everyone along with you. Vision must be focused. At times, even Jesus had to separate Himself from His disciples and go to a solitary place to pray and seek His Father (Mark 1:35–37). It was times of prayer and solitude with the Father that sustained Jesus through the process of vision fulfillment. Realize that it may be years before your vision is fulfilled. The book that I am writing today is the result of a decades-long dream and vision. Not long after the birth of Agape Divinity School, our school joined the Apostolic Council for Educational Accountability (ACEA), located in Colorado Springs, Colorado. For several years I represented our school at the annual conference. During one of our sessions, Peter Wagner invited those of us who desired to write books to allow him to lay hands on us and pray, as he has authored many, many books. That day Peter laid hands on me and spoke over my life. Now, a decade or so later I am publishing my first book. God told the prophet Habakkuk, "For the vision is for an appointed time … though it tarry, wait for it" (Habakkuk 2:3 KJV). God knows what circumstances we need to encounter to mature and unlock our measure of faith to the degree that it becomes a blessing to the body of Christ. People, life and situations become the pressure cooker that produces the maturity necessary to give birth to real vision.

The time is now. Don't put if off or procrastinate any longer. Although it may sound like a cliché, I believe there exists a people of God in the earth today who are ready to unlock their measure of faith and do great exploits never before seen in the earth.

> Do not call to mind the former things,
> Or ponder things of the past.
> Behold, I will do something new,
> Now it will spring forth;
> Will you not be aware of it?
> I will even make a roadway in the wilderness,
> Rivers in the desert.
> The beasts of the field will glorify Me;
> The jackals and the ostriches;
> Because I have given waters in the wilderness
> And rivers in the desert,
> To give drink to My chosen people.
> The people whom I formed for Myself,
> Will declare My praise.

— Isaiah 43:18–21

PRAYER OF SALVATION

I t's possible you are reading this book and have never asked Jesus Christ into your heart as your Lord and Savior. By repeating these words in faith and sincerity, you can invite Jesus into your life and receive salvation:

> Father God, I acknowledge that I am a sinner in need of salvation. I repent of my sins and surrender my life to Jesus Christ. I believe the gospel message that Jesus came to redeem me from a life of sin and bondage through His shed blood on the cross. Thank You for my new life in Christ and for making me a new creation.

Now that you are a believer, I want to encourage you to pray and ask God to lead you to a local church where you can be water baptized and introduced into discipleship. It is important that you seek out regular fellowship with believers of like faith in a Christ-centered, Bible-teaching, Spirit-filled and people-loving community.

Romans 10:9–10 "that if you confess with your mouth Jesus as Lord, and believe in your heart that God raised Him from the dead, you shall be saved; for with the heart man believes, resulting in righteousness, and with the mouth he confesses, resulting in salvation."

Suggested reading:
St. John Chapters 1–3
St. Matthew Chapters 5–8
Romans Chapter 10
II Corinthians Chapter 5
Ephesians Chapter 2

ENDNOTES

1 Bill Johnson, *Face to Face with God: The Ultimate Quest to Experience His Presence* (Lake Mary, FL., Charisma House, 2007), 93

2 Bill Hull, *Choose the Life: Exploring a Faith That Embraces Discipleship* (Grand Rapids, MI: Baker Books, 2004), 18

3 Stephen Everett, *God's Kingdom; Fulfilling God's Plan for Your Victory* (Shippensburg, PA, Destiny Image Publishers, Inc., 2005), 101

4 Michelangelo. (n.d.). BrainyQuote.com. Retrieved July 22, 2014, from BrainyQuote.com Web site: http://www.brainyquote.com/quotes/m/michelange137785.html

5 Derek Prince, *Faith to Live By* (New Kensington, PA Whitaker House, 1977), 11

6 Strong's, *Greek Dictionary,* Strong's Exhaustive Concordance of the Bible (Nashville: Abingdon, 1976), #5287

7 Strong's, *Greek Dictionary,* Strong's Exhaustive Concordance of the Bible (Nashville: Abingdon, 1976), #2540

8   Bill Johnson, *Face to Face With God* (Lake Mary, Florida, Charisma House, 2007), 122

9   James Strong, *Hebrew and Chaldee Dictionary,* Strong's Exhaustive Concordance of the Bible (Nashville: Abingdon, 1976), #6960

10   Stephen Everett, God's Kingdom: Fulfilling God's Plan for Your Victory (Shippensburg, PA., Destiny Image, Publishers, Inc., 2005), 104

11   Strong's, *Greek Dictionary*, Strong's Exhaustive Concordance of the Bible (Nashville: Abingdon, 1976), #4487

12   Bill Johnson, *Face to Face with God: The Ultimate Quest to Experience His Presence* (Lake Mary, FL., Charisma House, 2007), 196

13   Strong's, *Greek Dictionary*, Strong's Exhaustive Concordance of the Bible Nashville: Abingdon, 1976), #5449